GLOBAL QUESTIONS

Why do People Seek Asylum?

Cath Senker

W
FRANKLIN WATTS
LONDON • SYDNEY

First published in 2008 by Franklin Watts

Franklin Watts
338 Euston Road
London NW1 3BH

Franklin Watts Australia
Level 17/207 Kent Street, Sydney, NSW 2000

Produced by Arcturus Publishing Limited,
26/27 Bickels Yard, 151–153 Bermondsey Street, London SE1 3HA

Series concept: Alex Woolf
Editor: Nicola Barber
Designer: Ian Winton
Illustrator: Stefan Chabluk

Picture credits:
Corbis: cover (Fehim Demir/ epa), title page, 9, 20 and 38 (Reuters), 6 (Mohamed Messara/ epa), 7 (Mimi Mollica), 8 (Lynsey Addario), 13, 14 and 16 (Bettmann), 17 (Jean Louis Atlan/ Sygma), 18 (Maurizio Gambarini/ dpa), 21 (Jerome Sessini), 22 (JB Russell/ Sygma), 24 (Wang Ying/ Xinhua Press), 27 (Touhig Sion/ Corbis Sygma), 28 (Wolfgang Langenstrassen/ dpa), 30 (Andy Rain/ epa), 31 (epa), 32 (Robert Ghement/ epa), 35 (Alaa Badarneh/ epa), 37 (Ed Kashi), 41 (Ai Abbas/ epa), 43 (John Van Hasselt).
Topfoto: 40 (Hunter).

Cover caption: Kosovar Albanian refugees look out of the window of a bus as they arrive at a refugee camp in Macedonia, in April 1999.

The author would like to acknowledge the following sources: pp 6–7 Murad's story from 'In Europe, Iraqi Asylum-Seekers Find Doors Being Shut' by Sonia Phalnikar, Deutsche Welle, DW-WORLD.DE; p21 Na'all's story from 'Iraqi Refugee Voices: Stories of Desperation and Need', Refugees International, 20 July 2007; p25 Emmanuel Nyabera from UNHCR News Stories, 11 August 2006; p27 the Mustafas' story from BBC News, 10 May 1999; p29 Rwandan woman from 'Rwandan refugees in the UK', Information Centre about Asylum and Refuge in the UK, March 2004; p31 Sharon's story from 'Burmese army using rape to terrorise villagers' by Randeep Ramesh, Guardian Unlimited, 2 April 2007; p33 Ilona Ferkova's story from 'Memories of a Czech asylum seeker in Britain' by David Vaughan, Radio Prague, 2007; p35 Jevera's story from the PAIR Project, 2001; p36 asylum seeker figures from 2006 Global Trends: Refugees, Asylum-seekers, Returnees, Internally Displaced and Stateless Persons, UNHCR, 2007; p39 Afghan child's story from http://www.humanrights.gov.au/human_rights/children_detention_report/rep, HREOC, 2004; p42 'The Case for Environmental Refugees' by Andrew Simms, on the Green Cross Optimist website.

A CIP catalogue record for this book is available from the British Library.

Dewey Decimal Classification Number: 323.6'31

ISBN 978 0 7496 8219 4

Printed in China

Franklin Watts is a division of Hachette Children's Books, an Hachette Livre UK company.
www.hachettelivre.co.uk

Contents

Who are asylum seekers?

Most people do not want to leave their country – they go only in desperation. Choosing to escape is an incredibly difficult decision to make. When people run away, they leave behind their homes, their jobs and their relatives.

Running in fear

Murad Atshan is a 27-year-old film-maker from Baghdad, the capital of Iraq. In 2003, the US-led invasion of Iraq toppled the Iraqi dictator, Saddam Hussein. Baghdad descended into chaos. There was fighting between the Iraqis and the US forces that had occupied the country, as well as between different Iraqi groups. Every day, people were dying in violent bomb attacks. Murad fled to Germany, hoping to live a normal life in safety. When he arrived in Munich, he applied for asylum.

Yet in 2006, Murad's claim was rejected. The German authorities said that he didn't have a good enough reason to seek asylum. They argued that since Saddam Hussein had gone, Iraqis had nothing to fear and did not require asylum.

A fuel tanker burns in Baghdad after a car bomb set it on fire in 2005. There has been no peace in Iraq since Saddam Hussein was defeated by the US-led invasion in 2003.

This boat, which holds more than 300 migrants from Eritrea in eastern Africa, has just been spotted by Italian police as it approaches the island of Sicily. Each year, thousands of African migrants attempt to reach Europe.

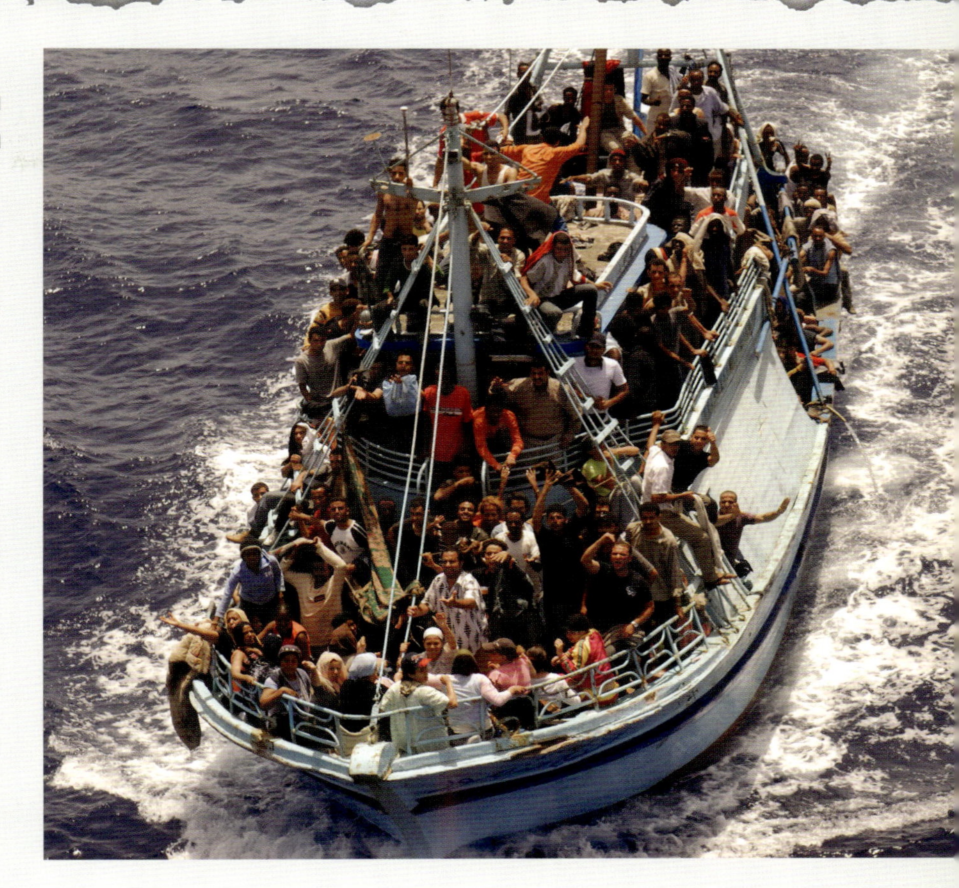

In 2007, while the authorities were considering what to do with him, Murad was living in a refugee centre in a small village. He was not allowed to leave the district or to work. His life was in limbo, his future uncertain. Life is often like this for asylum seekers.

Taking a risk

Refugees who wish to claim asylum often take huge risks. Running from a country in turmoil, many do not have an opportunity to get a passport or buy air tickets. Many refugees pay huge amounts of money to people-smugglers to organize long and dangerous journeys in secret. Refugees may have to walk hundreds of kilometres over land and through rivers, hide in the back of long-distance lorries, or survive hazardous sea voyages in tiny boats. They may not even know in which country they'll eventually arrive – if they survive at all. To have any chance of making an asylum claim, a person needs to be quick-thinking, courageous, resourceful – and to have a supply of cash.

Expert View

'Refugees are forced to leave their countries because they have been persecuted or have a well-founded fear of persecution. Refugees run away. They often do not know where they will end up. Refugees rarely have the chance to make plans for their departure such as packing their personal belongings or saying farewell to loved ones.'

United Nations High Commissioner for Refugees in the UK, 2003

These women, photographed in 2007, are sheltering in a camp for Internally Displaced Persons in Darfur, Sudan. Africans and Arabs in the region have left their homes in fear of violence at the hands of military groups allegedly backed by the Sudanese government.

Who are refugees and asylum seekers?

Refugees are people who escape from their country because of war or persecution. Most refugees leave quickly as a large group during an emergency and cross the border to the nearest safer country. They hope to return home when the situation has improved.

International law gives a more narrow definition of refugees. According to the United Nations (UN) Convention relating to the Status of Refugees (1951), refugees are people who have fled their country and cannot return to it because of a 'well-founded fear of persecution for reasons of race, religion, nationality, membership of a particular social group or political opinion'. This definition does not include people fleeing war or conflict in general. It is on the basis of this definition that refugees can claim asylum – the right to seek protection in another country. While refugees are waiting for a government to decide if they can stay in a particular country, they are known as asylum seekers.

Refugees or not?

Large groups of people escape war or persecution but stay within their own countries. They are known as Internally Displaced Persons (IDPs). Other people may not be counted as refugees even though they find themselves in similar situations. For example, neither the Kurds nor the Palestinians have a homeland. They are stateless peoples who live as minority groups in various countries.

A broad definition of refugees includes both IDPs and stateless people. An international organization called the United Nations High Commissioner for Refugees (UNHCR), which was set up in 1950, looks after all types of refugees.

Migrants

The vast majority of people who move to another country are not refugees – they are migrants who leave to escape poverty and seek a better life. Yet although they migrate as workers, they may also be moving to avoid persecution. For example, in Germany there are about 500,000 Kurdish people from Turkey. These Kurds came to Germany partly because it is a much wealthier country than Turkey and they can earn good money there. Yet persecution gave them an additional motive to migrate. Although things have improved a little over recent years, Kurdish people still do not have equal rights in Turkey.

> **FOCUS**
>
> **Twice uprooted, still no asylum**
>
> Fourteen-year-old Meltem, a Kurdish girl from Turkey, has had to grow up fast. When she was small, she and her parents fled Turkey for Germany to seek asylum. When their claim was rejected in 2001 they travelled to the UK. Then Meltem's father left them. Meltem and her mother settled in Doncaster, in northern England. A highly intelligent girl, Meltem learnt English quickly and became an outstanding student. At the same time, she studied asylum law to help the family's lawyers pursue their asylum claim. However, in November 2007, the government decided Meltem and her mother had no right to stay in the UK and should be sent back to Germany.

A Turkish clothes shop in the Kreuzberg district of Berlin, which is called 'Little Istanbul' because so many Turkish people live there. Turkish workers have been migrating to Germany to work since 1961.

Where are refugees and asylum seekers?

Most migrants move to wealthier countries. However, the majority of the world's refugees flee in large numbers from a crisis in one Less Economically Developed Country (LEDC) to a neighbouring safer one. The poorer countries are the source of most refugees, and they take most of them in, too. Countries in Africa and Asia receive four-fifths of the world's refugees.

At the end of 2006, Pakistan, Syria and Iran had the highest number of refugees. Between them, they hosted nearly one in three of all the refugees in the world.

Number of refugees and asylum seekers (2006)

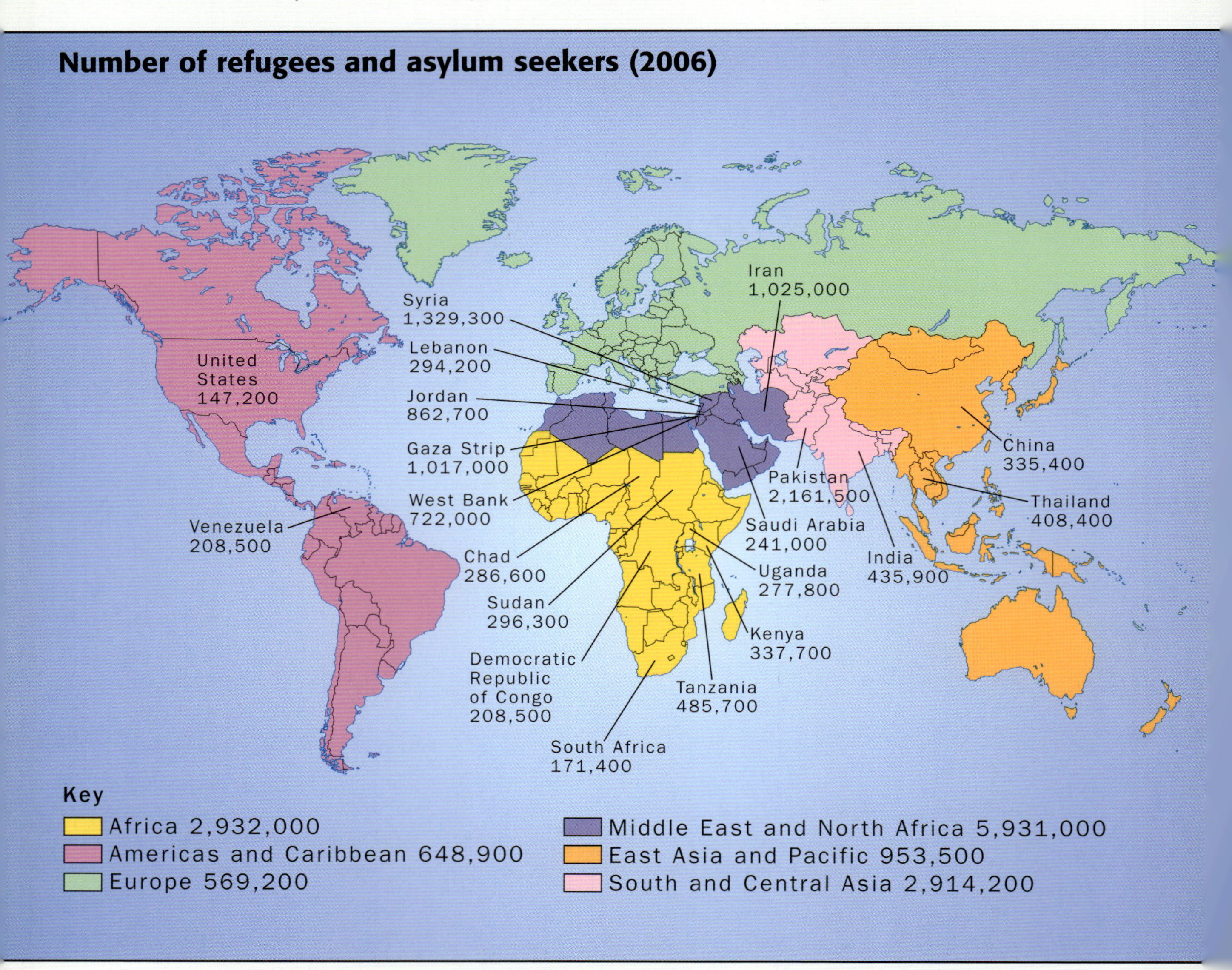

This world map shows where refugees and asylum seekers were found at the end of 2006. The individual countries that hosted the greatest number of refugees at that time are indicated.

FORUM

Should asylum seekers have the right to stay in a safer country for as long as they like?

'The possibility always exists that America from time to time may need to provide temporary first-asylum protection for larger numbers of refugees fleeing neighboring countries. But temporary asylum protection should not on humanitarian grounds increase the number of people permanently settling in the United States.'

Roy Beck, 'The Case Against Immigration', 1996

'Human Rights Watch believes the right to asylum is a matter of life and death and cannot be compromised. In our work to stop human rights abuses in countries around the world, we seek to address the root causes that force people to flee. We also advocate [push] for greater protection for refugees and IDPs and for an end to the abuses they suffer when they reach supposed safety.'

Human Rights Watch, 2006

Do you agree with either of these opinions?

Most of these refugees did not seek asylum as individuals but were accepted as a group. They crossed the border from Afghanistan, a neighbouring country that has suffered from conflict since 1979. Similarly, during the civil war that erupted in Rwanda in 1994, more than 2 million refugees escaped en masse to neighbouring Tanzania, Burundi and the Democratic Republic of Congo.

Claiming asylum

Only a minority of refugees worldwide make an individual claim to asylum. In 2006, there were 9.9 million refugees in the world, while worldwide 596,000 people applied for asylum. The total number of asylum seekers waiting for their claims to be processed was about 740,000. This figure includes the people who applied for asylum in 2006 as well as those who had applied in previous years and were still awaiting a decision. Asylum seekers, therefore, form just a fraction of the total number of refugees. Out of all the people cared for by UNHCR in 2006, refugees formed 30.1 per cent, while asylum seekers made up 2.3 per cent.

Have there always been asylum seekers?

Throughout history, people have fled their homes to escape natural disaster, persecution or war. In ancient times, a place of asylum was a safe building from which a person could not be forced to move. For example, in ancient Greece, a person who was being pursued by enemies and needed protection had the right to hide in a temple. When Christianity became widespread, churches became a place of sanctuary.

Forced to flee

At various times in history, groups of people have suffered persecution because they did not share the religion of the majority in society. In 1492, Christian forces completed their reconquest of the whole of Spain from Muslim rule. Despite the fact that Christians, Muslims and Jews had lived side by side for many centuries, the victorious rulers, King Ferdinand and Queen Isabella, were keen to unite Spain as a Christian country. They forced Jews and Muslims to choose between converting to Christianity or leaving Spain: many thousands of Jews and Muslims left.

Another example comes from France in the sixteenth and seventeenth centuries. France was a Catholic country, but a small minority, known as the Huguenots, followed the Protestant form of Christianity. During a series of religious wars,

FOCUS

Jewish refugees in China

In the early twentieth century, a few thousand Russian-Jewish refugees made their way to northern China. In the 1930s, after Japan invaded Manchuria, many moved again to Shanghai. There the Russian Jews rebuilt their community. They set up shops and restaurants and read Russian newspapers. There were seven synagogues for worship, and a music club where they listened to great European performers. The children went to a Jewish school and joined Jewish scout groups, football leagues and chess tournaments. In their free time, they cheered on Jewish boxers.

This illustration depicts the scene at a railway station as Jewish people, carrying whatever belongings they can, are expelled from St Petersburg, Russia, in 1885.

thousands of Huguenots lost their lives. In the late seventeenth century, around 400,000 Huguenots fled to England, Prussia, the Netherlands and America.

Restricting refugees

Until the late nineteenth century there were no laws to stop refugees from entering a country. At that time, major economic and political crises flared up in Russia and several eastern European countries. Many people in these countries blamed the Jewish populations for their problems – they believed that Jewish people were well-off at a time when others went hungry – and launched violent attacks on them. Between 1880 and 1929, more than 3.5 million Jewish people fled the persecution. Most headed for the United States and Western Europe. However, the governments of these Western countries became alarmed at the numbers of people arriving, and they started to bring in rules to control the influx of refugees. They toughened up these restrictions even further during the 1930s, when tens of thousands of Jewish people were desperate to escape from Nazi Germany.

Asylum in law

Although there have been laws restricting the movement of refugees for more than a century, the rules that allow people to claim asylum were not brought in until after World War II. Between 40 and 50 million people had died in the war, while a further 60 million people had been displaced from their homes. Afterwards, the international community was determined to prevent another devastating war and to protect human rights. In 1948, the UN proclaimed a Universal Declaration of

These German refugees had fled to Poland during World War II. In December 1945, they made their way back on foot to Berlin in eastern Germany. Of a group of 150 who had left Lodz two months earlier, these were the only survivors.

Human Rights. It stated that all human beings have the right to live in freedom and safety, whatever their race, gender or way of life; and that they have the right to believe in what they want, including the religion of their choice.

The declaration did not, however, include the legal right to demand asylum, and countries were not obliged to grant it. The same is true of the 1951 convention (see page 8) which stated that governments had to allow asylum seekers a fair chance to explain why they needed a safe haven, but that asylum was not a right.

There have been attempts to bring in a right of asylum but they have failed. For example, the UN Declaration on Territorial Asylum (1967) included the rule of 'non-refoulement' – not sending people back to a country where they would be in danger. Yet there were important exceptions, such as in cases where it was judged that allowing the person to stay could harm the security of the host nation. Under asylum law, it remains the case that individuals have to prove that they were persecuted in order to obtain asylum.

Expert View

Professor George J. Andreopoulos explains that the right to asylum is not part of international law:

'...the Universal Declaration of Human Rights (UDHR), which, though recognizing (article 14) the right "to seek and to enjoy in other countries asylum from persecution," does not explicitly [clearly] provide a right of asylum. The original draft of that article, which referred to the individual's right "to seek and to be granted asylum from persecution," would have afforded more protection to asylum seekers.'

Professor George J. Andreopoulos, 2008

Decades of conflict

The international community's hopes for peace after World War II were soon dashed. Since 1945 there have been more than 150 further wars. Between the 1950s and 1970s, many countries in Asia and Africa fought wars of independence against their European rulers. During the 1950s, Morocco, Tunisia and Algeria in North Africa all struggled for independence from France. Morocco and Tunisia achieved liberation in 1956 but the French continued a long, bloody war in Algeria. The Algerians finally became independent in 1962. These conflicts forced large numbers of people to flee. In the late 1950s many Algerians left for neighbouring Morocco and Tunisia, hoping to return in calmer times.

After the communists defeated the South Vietnamese and their US allies, many South Vietnamese tried to escape the country. These civilians are climbing on to a bus going to the US embassy, from where they will leave Vietnam.

The Cold War

Although most of the former colonies eventually became independent, new causes of aggression arose. After World War II, the United States and the Soviet Union (USSR) became rival superpowers. The two countries sought influence in the world by backing opposite sides in various conflicts. In Vietnam, for example, communists allied to the USSR fought against the South Vietnamese government, which was linked to the United States. In 1975, the whole of Vietnam came under control of the communists after the defeat of the South Vietnamese. Many anti-communist Vietnamese left as refugees.

In the 1980s, the United States became concerned that under the rule of the left-wing Sandinista National Liberation Front (Sandinistas), the Central American country of Nicaragua was turning towards communism. The US government backed a force called the Contras to oppose the government. The conflict between the Sandinistas and the Contras resulted in a civil war that lasted the entire decade, and caused continual flows of refugees and displaced people. In 1990 a new government was elected that reversed the Sandinistas' left-wing policies.

Forced migrations

In the 1990s, warfare led to some of the largest forced migrations of refugees in history. The break-up of Yugoslavia in the early 1990s resulted in several wars and massive waves of refugees. During the same decade, millions of Afghans moved to Iran and Pakistan to avoid civil war between rival regional leaders in their own country. In 1994, the genocide in Rwanda (see pages 28-9) forced more than 2 million people to escape. Wars have always created refugees and asylum seekers.

FORUM

In the 1930s, there was debate in both the United States and Britain over whether to accept Jewish refugees from Nazi Germany:

'To be ruled by misguided sentimentalism would be disastrous. Once it was known that Britain offered sanctuary to all who cared to come, the floodgates would be opened and we would be inundated [flooded] by thousands seeking a home.'

Daily Mail*, 28 March 1938*

'Here is a chance of taking the young generation of a great people, here is a chance of mitigating [reducing] to some extent the terrible suffering of their parents and their friends.'

British Foreign Minister Samuel Hoare, 21 November 1938, having persuaded the government to rescue thousands of Jewish children

Do you think it was right for the UK to take in Jewish refugees?

These soldiers are members of the Sandinista army. They defended the Nicaraguan government from the Contras during the 1980s.

How does warfare create asylum seekers?

The statistics show that war remains the most common reason for flight in the early twenty-first century. In 2006, the highest number of refugees came from Afghanistan, Iraq, Somalia, the Democratic Republic of Congo and Burundi. The greatest numbers of asylum seekers came from Somalia, Iraq and Zimbabwe. These are all countries where there has been serious conflict over many years and where there are still problems.

In several African countries, military groups boost their numbers by forcing young boys to become soldiers. These child soldiers with rifles in their hands are fighters in the Democratic Republic of Congo.

Modern wars

In the past, wars were usually fought between armies on a battlefield. Modern wars, however, are fought in the cities, towns and villages where ordinary people live. They affect whole populations. Civilians regularly get caught in the crossfire and are killed or wounded. Modern missiles are aimed at military targets and important buildings, but they frequently miss, hitting homes and schools instead. Even if civilians are not being attacked, armies seize their resources to fight the war. As they move around a country, soldiers take over buildings, food and water supplies from local people.

Expert View

'At the heart of the conflict is a struggle for DRC's vast reserves of gold, diamonds and other natural resources. ... Military and political leaders have used their position to exploit these resources and large-scale human rights violations such as the mass killing of civilians, rape and other forms of torture have been committed by government forces, armed opposition factions and foreign troops in the war for profit.'

Amnesty International, 2005

Crisis in the Congo

The Democratic Republic of Congo (DRC) experienced a devastating war between 1998 and 2003. DRC is a huge country, rich in natural resources including diamonds, copper and coltan (used in the production of mobile phones). The war involved several other African countries. The government of DRC was backed by Angola, Chad, Namibia, Sudan and Zimbabwe as it fought a rebel force that was supported by Uganda and Rwanda. All the sides in the war have been accused of fighting in order to gain a share of DRC's vast wealth. Human rights organizations have alleged that Western companies also became involved in order to exploit the country's resources.

Around 4 million people lost their lives during the conflict, and millions were forcibly displaced or escaped the country. The majority of deaths were not caused directly by the fighting. Most victims died of hunger or disease because they could not find enough food, water and medicines to survive. The conflict continued after the ceasefire in 2003 and, despite a peace pact signed in January 2008, seemed likely to continue. In 2007 there were still 410,000 refugees from DRC, mostly in the neighbouring countries of the Central African Republic, Republic of Congo, Tanzania and Sudan. The fighting after 2003 also created new waves of IDPs. The casualties in the DRC war have been so shocking that some people have called it Africa's 'First World War'.

As Afghans heard the news of the likely US-led invasion of their country in November 2001, many fled towards Pakistan. This picture shows Afghans waiting at a border crossing which has been closed by Pakistan to prevent more refugees entering the country.

Foreign invasion: Afghanistan...

Sometimes, war is launched on a country from outside. A foreign invasion creates mass panic. People may be frantic to leave, fearing the battles to come between the attackers and the defenders of their country. In 1979, tens of thousands of troops from the Soviet Union (USSR) invaded Afghanistan to support a pro-communist government. A major civil war broke out between the Soviet forces and anti-communist fighters. During the 1980s, 6 million Afghans – one-fifth of the population – fled the country, mainly to nearby Pakistan and Iran.

The Soviet troops abandoned Afghanistan in 1989, but the war carried on between different military groups. In the early 1990s, after law and order broke down completely, an extreme Islamic party called the Taliban came to power. In 2001, US-led forces led another invasion to topple the Taliban. Once more, Afghans fled their land.

...and Iraq

After changing the government of Afghanistan, the United States turned to Iraq. In 2003, a US-led invasion overthrew the Iraqi dictator Saddam Hussein and occupied Iraq. However, the new government attracted little support, and violent struggles erupted. Iraqis fought against the American occupation of their country, while different

Iraqi groups also battled against each other. The war made daily life almost impossible in large areas of the country. Iraqis lacked jobs, regular clean water and electricity supplies. Prices for basic foods and fuel rocketed, and the fighting made it extremely dangerous to go to school, college or work. In 2006, Iraqis formed the second largest group of both refugees (1.5 million) and asylum seekers (34,200) worldwide. In 2007, their numbers swelled to 2.2 million as the situation in their country grew even worse. Meanwhile, another 2.2 million people moved to safer places within Iraq.

FOCUS

Na'all, a boy at work

Thirteen-year-old schoolboy Na'all fled Baghdad for Damascus in Syria with his family in 2003. Since living in Damascus, he hasn't been able to go to school. He has found a job so that his mum can look after his disabled father and grandmother. Na'all is working illegally in a hotel because Iraqi refugees aren't allowed to work. He earns less than a Syrian would, but is grateful for the job. Na'all is losing his chance to have an education, but as his mum says, "Who else will pay our rent? Who else will pay for water and food?"

Iraqi refugees wait patiently outside a refugee centre in Damascus, Syria, in order to be registered. In 2007, more than 1 million Iraqis sought refuge in neighbouring Syria.

Most Iraqi refugees made their way to nearby Jordan and Syria. They stayed with friends or relatives, or found shelter in refugee camps. As one Iraqi journalist said, 'Iraqis who are unable to flee the country are now in a queue, waiting their turn to die.'

Arriving as asylum seekers

A tiny minority of refugees manage to reach a country where they can make an individual asylum claim – usually a More Economically Developed Country (MEDC). Sometimes an asylum seeker may make a claim before reaching the country to which he or she wants to go, but this isn't simple. For example, Iraqis who wish to claim asylum in the United States cannot claim asylum from inside Iraq. They must make an expensive and risky journey to a neighbouring

Hidden in the back of a truck, four Romanian migrants hoped to remain undiscovered until they reached the UK. Unluckily for them, French officials in Calais have found their hiding place.

FORUM

Some argue that people should be free to move wherever they like, while others believe countries have the right to keep out people they do not want.

'I think freedom of movement is one of the most basic human rights, as anyone who is denied it can confirm. It is abhorrent [wrong for moral reasons] that the rich and the educated are allowed to circulate [move] around the world more or less freely, while the poor are not – causing, in effect, a form of global apartheid [separation].'

UK economist and journalist Philippe Legrain

'France can only remain generous if those who are here in violation of our rights and our laws [those who break our laws] are returned home.'

French Interior Minister Nicolas Sarkozy,* Libération, *6 June 2005

Do you think there should be freedom of movement?

country before they can seek asylum. They have to survive on their savings while waiting to see if their claim is accepted. In 2007, 1,608 Iraqis succeeded in being resettled in the United States.

Generally, refugees travel to a safer country so they can claim asylum on arrival. Many refugees are forced to travel to this new country illegally because they are unable to use a legal route (see page 7).

Different destinations

The destination of refugees varies from year to year depending on the conflicts at that time and how easy it is for people to reach a country where they can claim asylum. In 2006 the continent of Europe had the highest number of asylum claims, followed by Africa. The main destination country for new asylum seekers in 2006 was South Africa. It is the richest country in Africa and is close to several major conflict regions, especially Zimbabwe. The second main country for asylum applications was the United States, followed by Kenya, France, the UK, Sweden and Canada. It is important to remember, though, that while around 600,000 people made their first claim for asylum in 2006, there were 9.9 million refugees in total, mostly in LEDCs.

Chapter 4

Why does civil war cause so many to flee?

Civil wars cause huge waves of refugees, IDPs and asylum seekers because the conflict occurs within the population of a country. Civil wars divide people by political beliefs, religion or ethnic group. They may set neighbour against neighbour and even split up families. People from one group may be attacked by an opposition group, or simply become caught up in the fighting.

Women walk past ruined buildings in Mogadishu, the capital of Somalia, in 2007. Sixteen years of conflict have destroyed what was once a beautiful city.

Somalia

The major civil wars since the 1990s have tended to occur in LEDCs. One example is Somalia. There has been no strong central government since 1991, when President Siad Barre was overthrown. The groups that toppled him could not agree on a replacement government and began to fight among themselves.

In 1992 the fighting stopped food aid from being distributed around Somalia, and around half a million Somalis starved to death. After further years of conflict a new government was established in 2000, but it was unable to unite the warring groups. In 2006, an Islamic organization gained control of a large part of southern Somalia. The government fought back, with Ethiopian support, and the violence increased once again.

The long civil war has forced hundreds of thousands to leave as refugees, IDPs and asylum seekers. In 2007 there were about half a million Somali refugees and around a million IDPs. By the end of 2007, renewed fighting between government and Islamist forces had reduced the Somali capital Mogadishu to a ghost town. Around two-thirds of the city's residents had fled, many to neighbouring provinces. About 335,000 Somali refugees were in refugee camps in Kenya, Ethiopia and Yemen, afraid to return, while a small number sought asylum in the United States, UK and the Netherlands.

A new life in the United States

Since 1991, tens of thousands of Somalis have resettled in the United States, forming the largest African refugee group in the country. Around 12,000 of them are Somali Bantu, an ethnic minority that suffered persecution within Somalia. The Bantu were frequently denied land and education. The civil war made things even worse because none of the warring groups protected the Bantu. Even after they escaped to Kenya and lived in refugee camps, the Bantu were treated badly by other Somalis. After several years of waiting, they were finally admitted to the United States.

Expert View

'The continuing influx of Somalis to Dadaab [a refugee camp in Kenya] is affecting morale among long-term residents of the camps, including some who have been here for almost 14 years. In October 2004, the refugees at Dadaab were full of hope after Somalia elected a president and put a government in place for the first time in 15 years. UNHCR began initial preparations to take the refugees back home, but the renewed fighting has dashed these hopes.'

Emmanuel Nyabera, Dadaab, Kenya, UNHCR, 2006

Ethnic conflict

As the case of the Somali Bantu shows, sometimes there is conflict between people from different ethnic groups within the same country. The group that has the upper hand may push out its enemies, forcing them to leave as refugees or IDPs. This also happened in Europe in the 1990s.

The end of Yugoslavia

Yugoslavia was a communist country made up of six republics. The population was a mix of different ethnic groups, including Serbs, Croats, Muslims and Albanians. In 1990, the communist government fell. Yugoslavia divided into separate republics, which fought each other for land and control. Slobodan Milosevic was the president of Yugoslavia from 1989 and leader of Serbia, the most powerful of the republics. He promised to increase the size of Serbia to include Serbs who lived in other republics. Serbia fought a war against Croatia in 1991 and against Bosnia in 1995. Milosevic seized territory, but was forced by both Croatia and Bosnia to return it.

Meanwhile, the Kosovar Albanians – Albanian people living in the republic of Kosovo – protested against Milosevic's government. They wanted independence from Serbia, which controlled Kosovo. Some Kosovars formed the Kosovo Liberation Army to fight Serbia. Violence broke out between the two sides in 1998, forcing 350,000 Kosovar

The map on the left shows the former Yugoslav Federation in 1991. On the right, the map indicates the separate republics in 2008.

A raid by the Serb army in June 1998 forced these Kosovars to flee their homes and seek refuge in the mountains. As the weather grew colder in the autumn, displaced people living in the open air had to find shelter in urban areas.

Albanians to flee as refugees and IDPs. In April 1999, after peace talks failed, NATO bombed Serbia and Kosovo to make Milosevic withdraw from Kosovo.

Ethnic cleansing

The Serbs took violent revenge on the Kosovar Albanians in the form of 'ethnic cleansing' – forcing the Albanians to leave Kosovo. More than 750,000 Kosovar Albanians escaped as refugees to Albania, Bosnia and Montenegro, while around 700,000 went into hiding in the remote forests and mountains of Kosovo. Tens of thousands of Kosovars sought asylum in another European country. In June 1999 NATO bombing stopped and a peace agreement was signed. After the conflict, 95 per cent of the refugees returned to Kosovo. Going back was difficult. Many found their houses and communities destroyed, and they risked death or injury from landmines – small explosive devices that lie on or just under the ground. Nevertheless, they were relieved to be home.

FOCUS

The Mustafas flee Kosovo

Mr Mustafa worked as a factory administrator near Ferzaj in Kosovo. During the Kosovo War, Serb police ordered him and his family to leave their village. He described what happened: "They came into the house and they asked us for money and they said if we didn't give them money they would take our lives ... I left my parents, two brothers and a sister – there is no life over there. The only thing you can see is terror from the military and paramilitary groups. You can't organize your private life." Mr Mustafa, his wife and four small children fled to the relative safety of a refugee camp. Then they were flown to Scotland, where they were offered asylum for a year.

Genocide in Rwanda

Even more devastating than ethnic cleansing, genocide is the attempt to wipe out an entire ethnic group. This happened in Rwanda, in central Africa, in the 1990s.

Before Rwanda became an independent country in 1962, it was ruled as a colony by Germany and then by Belgium. The country's colonial rulers encouraged rivalry between the minority Tutsi and the majority Hutu people because it made it easier to keep control. They gave education and better jobs to the Tutsis so that they could help to run the colony. The Hutus resented this unfair treatment.

When Rwanda gained its independence, the Hutus took power. Yet the tensions between Tutsis and Hutus continued, and in 1994 they exploded into violence after the Hutu president was killed. Hutu soldiers went on the rampage, killing around 1.5 million Tutsis, along with any Hutus who didn't support them. The killings were brutal. The soldiers stripped their victims and hacked them to pieces with big, heavy knives – or beat them to death with clubs. Even babies were not spared.

These are photographs of victims of the genocide in Kigali, Rwanda. Although the political situation stabilized after Rwanda was torn apart by the massacres, the country remains one of the poorest in the world.

In fear of their lives, hundreds of thousands of Tutsis left for the neighbouring countries of Tanzania and Zaire (now the Democratic Republic of Congo). Then Tutsi forces gained control of Rwanda, and about 2 million Hutus fled to Zaire. Many of them had been involved in the genocide and now feared revenge attacks.

Rwandan refugees

While the vast majority of refugees escaped to neighbouring countries, a small minority sought asylum further afield. Around 5,750 Rwandans sought asylum in 19 European countries between 1990 and 1997. More than half of them were granted asylum.

Following the hideous massacres, a new government was formed that included both Hutus and Tutsis. It promised refugees that it was safe to return to their country – and most did. Some were forced by Tanzania to go back, while others chose to return home. Over the next few years, with great efforts from the Rwandan people, the country became stable again. Yet the survivors remain haunted by their horrific experiences. As one young woman who claimed asylum in the UK after the genocide explained, "Those who survived have nothing to look back to. We are constantly living in the shadow of the genocide . . . many scarred for life physically, mentally and psychologically."

FORUM

Some people argue that it is right for countries to use military force in another country to stop genocide, while others disagree.

'War often carries enormous human costs, but we recognize that the imperative [importance] of stopping or preventing genocide or other systematic slaughter can sometimes justify the use of military force. For that reason, Human Rights Watch has on rare occasion advocated humanitarian intervention – for example, to stop ongoing genocide in Rwanda and Bosnia.'

Human Rights Watch, 2004

'When nations send their military forces into other nations' territory, it is rarely (if ever) for "humanitarian" purposes. They are typically pursuing their narrow national interest – grabbing territory, gaining geo-strategic advantage [political influence in that area], or seizing control of precious natural resources.'

Global Policy Forum, 2007

Do you think it is ever right to send military forces into another country?

Chapter 5

What's the link with human rights?

Wars are not the only reason that people seek asylum. Some people leave their countries because of violations of their human rights. These human rights were laid out in 1948 by the United Nations (see pages 14–15), but not all countries respect them.

No democracy

In some countries, people who oppose the government are not allowed to speak out. Individuals who write about their concerns in a newspaper, organize meetings or go to protests, might be put in prison – or worse.

Burma has had a military government (run by the army) since 1962. This government has a terrible reputation for abusing human rights. It is particularly vicious towards people from ethnic minority groups, such as the Karen and the Chin. Soldiers seize people and oblige them to work for the army like slaves. They murder, arrest and torture villagers to keep the Burmese population in fear. Even children are attacked, and according to Human Rights Watch, some are forced to become child soldiers.

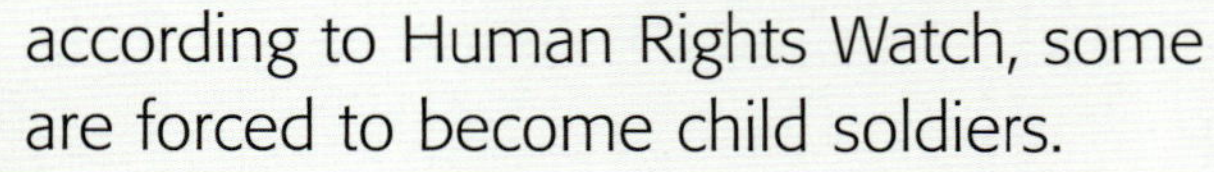

Pro-democracy Burmese protesters wear Aung San Suu Kyi masks at a demonstration in London in 2007.

No free speech

People in Burma are not permitted to speak out against the government. The military authorities check every magazine and newspaper to make sure there are no articles that criticize the government. They also control the TV and radio stations. The Burmese people listen to

Buddhist monks in Mumbai, India, hold a demonstration against the Burmese government. They are supporting the upsurge of protests in favour of democracy that erupted in Burma itself in 2007.

international radio stations – even though this is illegal – to find out what is really happening in the world. Members of the National League for Democracy (NLD), a political party that campaigns for democracy in Burma, are often arrested. The NLD's world-famous leader, Aung San Suu Kyi, has lived under house arrest for 12 years, unable to leave her home.

FOCUS

Sharon: lucky to work

Sharon is from the Chin people, a mostly Christian ethnic group in Burma, where the official religion is Buddhism. The army attacks the Chin because it says they are against the government. One day, Burmese soldiers came to Sharon's house to demand food. Then they raped her and dragged her away to work for them. After she was raped again, she ran away to India. Three years later, she lives with her two teenage daughters in one tiny room. Unlike most Burmese, Sharon is lucky because she has refugee status and is allowed to work. "I cannot speak the language here and there is a lot of discrimination against us because we are not Indian. But it is better here than in Burma," she says.

It is no surprise that around 3 million Burmese people have run away to other countries. The majority of these refugees are in Thailand, Malaysia, India and Bangladesh – poor countries that struggle to cope with the newcomers. Thailand makes life difficult for those that arrive; of about 2 million Burmese in Thailand, only 140,000 are recognized as refugees. The rest have to pay bribes to avoid being arrested as 'illegal aliens' and deported. Yet if there is no move towards democracy in Burma, the Burmese will continue to flee.

Ethnic minorities: the Roma

Even in democratic countries, where voters elect the government, people from particular ethnic minorities may be treated unfairly. This is often the case for the Roma. Around 9 million Roma live in Europe, mostly in eastern European countries.

The Roma used to be nomadic, travelling from place to place in caravans. They spoke their own Romani language and lived by their own customs. Nowadays, many Roma are

These Roma women and girls in Romania attend lessons at their village school to learn to read and write. The lessons form part of a special programme to improve Roma literacy levels.

settled in houses, but they cling on to their language and culture.

The Roma often suffer cruel persecution, especially in eastern European countries such as Poland, the Czech Republic and Romania. In Romania, they are the largest ethnic minority – and the poorest. They mostly live in overcrowded homes and about half of Roma adults are unemployed. It is hard for Roma children to enrol at school because they are rarely welcomed, and those who brave the classroom often suffer racism. The Roma regularly face racist violence, but frequently the police don't help them. In fact, the police themselves are sometimes involved in the attacks.

FOCUS

Ilona: I had to go

Romani writer Ilona Ferkova explains why she left the Czech Republic to seek asylum in the UK: "They wouldn't leave me alone. First came the foul letters, and then there were those phone calls to my husband. I couldn't go on any more. I'd told the police everything! And what did they do? Nothing! They said I should tell them who it was, then they'd be able to do something. Some good that did! I couldn't tell them something I didn't know myself! ... I had a job working with Roma mothers and children. It was good work. Some people didn't like the fact that I was working at the school as a teacher. They didn't want me to be there. That's why they sent those awful letters that struck terror into me."

Despite this persecution, it is hard for Roma to claim asylum because they come from countries that are supposedly democratic.

Indigenous people under pressure

Indigenous people also tend to suffer persecution. They are the people who originally lived in a country before new settlers arrived. In Brazil, for example, there are around 600,000 indigenous peoples from more than 200 groups. According to Brazilian law they have the right to live on their land in the traditional way. Yet, in practice, much of their land has been taken away, and the government does not provide adequate hospitals, clinics and schools for their communities. These groups also lose land to new farmers who are themselves moving from overcrowded areas, or to gold miners. All these problems are good reasons for people to seek refuge elsewhere. However, the poorest, most downtrodden people in society rarely have enough money to leave and seek asylum in another land.

No homeland: the Palestinians

Some of the largest groups of refugees in the world do not have a country of their own. When the State of Israel was established in Palestine in 1948, a bitter war flared up between Israel and the neighbouring Arab countries. Around 750,000 Palestinians fled as refugees from Israel to the neighbouring West Bank, Gaza Strip, Syria, Lebanon and Jordan. Israel did not permit them to return.

By 2007, there were 4.4 million Palestinian refugees in the Middle East, plus 1.5 million elsewhere in the world. This figure includes those who originally left Palestine, and their children and grandchildren. They are counted as refugees because the Palestinians have no homeland. Two-thirds of Palestinians in the Middle East live in other Arab countries. One-third – about 1.3 million people – remain in refugee camps in neighbouring countries or in the West Bank and Gaza Strip (occupied by Israel since 1967). In their hearts, they still hope to return home one day.

In the refugee camps, Palestinians lead tough lives. A high proportion have no job and rely on aid to survive. The camps are overcrowded, their homes are cramped, and they lack basic services such as roads and sewers. It's common to see raw sewage flowing in the narrow streets, where children play.

Refugees twice over

Since 1948, there has been a struggle between Israel and the Palestinian organizations in the West Bank and Gaza Strip. These organizations want to win back their homeland and

FORUM

A few people argue there should be no immigration controls at all, while others believe they are essential.

'No One Is Illegal UK challenges the ideology [theory] of immigration controls and campaigns for their total abolition. We oppose controls in principle and reject any idea there can be "fair" or "just" or "reasonable" or "non racist" controls. We make no distinction between "economic migrants" and "refugees", between the "legal" and the "illegal".'

' ... since we adopted very tough border protection policies in 2001, the number of people trying to come here illegally has virtually dried up.'

John Howard, Australian prime minister 1996–2007, who believed it was vital to prevent asylum seekers from arriving in Australia

Should there be immigration controls or not?

Israel has established military checkpoints all over the West Bank and the Gaza Strip so that its soldiers can stop the free movement of Palestinians who intend to carry out attacks on Israelis. However, the checkpoints also make it extremely hard for ordinary Palestinians to travel for work or study.

achieve essential human rights, but there is conflict within the Palestinian community itself about the best way to do this. The continuing turmoil has forced some Palestinians to flee once more and seek asylum in other countries.

Jevera is one of these people. A Palestinian school student from the West Bank, he featured in a documentary about how the conflict between Palestine and Israel affects children in both places. Jevera argued for peace between young Israelis and Palestinians. For this, he was threatened by one of the Palestinian liberation organizations. In fear of his life, he fled the West Bank for the United States, where he received asylum. Jevera continues his peace campaign by giving talks at universities about how to improve relations between Palestinians and Israelis.

What happens to asylum seekers?

When asylum seekers arrive in a new country, most will meet with mixed reactions. Some people welcome them, while others do not. The issue of asylum has caused great anxiety in MEDCs, the countries where most individual claims to asylum are made. Most Western governments express fears about the numbers of asylum seekers entering their countries. They worry that there will not be enough housing, school places or hospital beds because of increases in their populations. The media generally reflect these views, and many people agree. Because of these concerns, governments have introduced laws to restrict the numbers given asylum.

However, organizations that support asylum seekers argue on moral grounds that it is wrong to limit the number accepted. If people have been persecuted, they should be given refuge. They also point out that asylum seekers form a tiny proportion of the total population in MEDCs. The table below shows countries with the highest number of people seeking asylum and the proportion of the population they formed in 2006.

Country	Number of asylum seekers	Total population	Percentage of population
South Africa	53,400	47,390,900	0.11
USA	50,800	300,000,000	0.16
Kenya	37,300	34,707,817	0.10
France	30,800	60,876,136	0.05
UK	27,800	60,587,000	0.04
Sweden	24,300	9,107,420	0.26
Canada	22,900	32,547,200	0.07

In the United States, the Refugee Resettlement Program helps refugees to settle into their new communities. Thanks to a successful programme in Nashville, Tennessee, this high school has students from many different backgrounds.

Although most individual claims to asylum are made in MEDCs, a significant number are also made in LEDCs. As the chart shows, South Africa and Kenya were major destinations for asylum seekers in 2006. These countries are close to other African countries that are in the depths of serious conflict. For example, of the 53,400 people who claimed asylum in South Africa, 18,000 were from neighbouring Zimbabwe. As in MEDCs, there are arguments within these societies about whether or not asylum seekers should be welcomed.

Do asylum seekers commit crime?

There are other aspects to the debate over asylum seekers. Some people think that many asylum seekers are criminals. However, research has shown that asylum seekers are more likely to be victims of crime than to commit offences. A report from South Africa showed that they have a higher chance than local people of suffering crime and abuse at the hands of criminals, the police, employers and the general population.

Expert View

'Despite the misgivings of many South African leaders and citizens, the presence of non-citizens in South Africa should be seen as a testament to [evidence of] South Africa's prosperity [wealth], stability, and commitment to protecting the human rights of all people. In many instances, non-nationals make important contributions to South Africa's economy: by bringing valuable skills, capital [investing money], and a willingness to work.'

Consortium for Refugees and Migrants in South Africa, 2007

It is a common belief that many asylum seekers are not genuine refugees but have come to take advantage of the host country's welfare system. Yet those who support asylum seekers point out that most of them don't know anything about the welfare system in the host country before they arrive. They often have excellent skills and qualifications, and are keen to work for their living and contribute to society.

Showing they have suffered

People seeking asylum have to provide evidence that they are genuine, demonstrating that they have suffered from persecution, and would be in mortal danger if they returned to their country. But many asylum seekers do not even

The Australian government has an extremely strict policy towards asylum seekers. However, some Australians oppose the detention policy. These protesters gathered at Baxter Detention Centre in 2003 to express their opposition.

FOCUS

An Afghan in Australia

This Afghan child asylum seeker spent time in an Australian detention centre until his claim was accepted: "I want to tell you that actually I spent about fifteen nights in the ride to Australia. I was in a small boat if you want to call that a boat, because it was smaller than that, with lots of difficulties. When I saw [we were] getting near Australia I was becoming a little bit hopeful. When we passed Darwin I got to the detention centre; as soon as I looked at these barbed wires my mind was full of fear. That was the time that I experienced fear . . . When after all the negative experiences that I had in the detention centre, when I was released I felt like a normal human being and I felt that I was coming back to life!"

have passports or personal documents. Sometimes they cannot even prove which country they come from.

Winners and losers

The conditions for winning asylum have become harder in many countries. In Spain and Portugal, for example, the requirements for accepting asylum claims were tightened up in 2005. If an official thinks that an asylum seeker's story contains anything false or difficult to believe, or any outdated information, the claim can be turned down. This means that asylum seekers who have been persecuted can be refused simply because the official doesn't believe their stories.

Whether people obtain asylum also depends on where they come from. For example, the UK government has a list of countries that it believes are safe. If an asylum seeker comes from a country on that list, he or she is unlikely to receive asylum. This is why it is difficult for Roma from eastern European countries to gain asylum in the UK.

Detention centres

Asylum seekers are not allowed to work while their claim is being processed. They receive differing amounts of support, depending on the host country. In some countries, asylum seekers are sent to detention centres – secure places, like prisons. They have to stay there until they find out if they will be permitted to stay or not. In Australia, all asylum seekers are put in detention centres, while in the United States they are detained if the government believes they have entered the country illegally. European countries also detain some refugees.

Child asylum seekers

Some children travel alone to seek asylum. They may be escaping from child labour – being forced to work – or to avoid having to join an army. Some girls leave because of forced marriages or prostitution. But even unaccompanied children may be sent to detention centres. In the United States, around 7,000 unaccompanied children were placed in detention centres in 2006. According to the human rights organization Amnesty International, nearly half of them were placed in detention centres with young offenders (criminals). They often did not receive proper medical care or education. They found it extremely difficult to seek legal help to make their asylum claim. It's hard enough for adults to do this!

Deported or disappearing

Asylum seekers whose claims are refused may be deported because they don't have permission to stay in the country. However, many 'failed' asylum seekers are too terrified to return home. Instead, they 'disappear' into society, and live hidden from the authorities. Living in fear of discovery, they cannot use local services, such as the doctor or dentist, and their children can no longer go to school. It's a harsh life, but many refugees consider that it's better than what they face back home.

Resettlement and return

Asylum seekers whose claims are accepted can stay in the country. They have refugee status. Once their country is safer, refugees usually want to go home. In 2006, about 734,000 refugees worldwide chose to return to their homeland. However, if the conflict continues in their country for many years, they may remain in the host country and build a new life there.

The British government locks up asylum seekers it believes will 'disappear' if not detained. This detention centre, surrounded by a high barbed-wire fence, is in Dungavel, Scotland.

Although their country is still unsafe, many Iraqi refugees cannot afford to stay abroad. These refugees returned from Syria in late 2007. They are in Baghdad, waiting to collect money from the government to help them to resettle.

FORUM

The Australian government argues that it is necessary to place asylum seekers in detention, while human rights campaigners disagree.

'Australia's Migration Act 1958 requires people who are not Australian citizens and who are unlawfully in Australia to be detained. ... This requirement reflects Australia's right to determine who is permitted to enter and remain in Australia. ... Immigration detention is not used to punish people. It is an administrative [organizational] function whereby people who do not have a valid visa [permission to enter] are detained while their claims to stay are considered.'

Australian government website

'Many are imprisoned behind razor wire in some of the most hostile terrain [land] on earth, deliberately isolated from population centres in "detention centres" run by an American company specializing in top-security prisons. In their desperation, the refugees, many of them unaccompanied children, have resorted to suicide, starvation, arson [lighting fires] and mass escapes.'

Campaigning journalist John Pilger

Do you think asylum seekers should be detained?

What is the future for asylum seekers?

As long as war and persecution continue, refugees and asylum seekers will flee their homelands. Some conflicts will be resolved, others will continue and new ones will break out. The countries of origin and the countries of asylum will vary accordingly.

Environmental refugees

Some experts point to the growing problem of 'environmental refugees'. They foresee that millions of people will have to flee environmental disasters made more severe by climate change – including drought, floods and hurricanes. If the international community works to reduce the effects of climate change, perhaps fewer people will lose their homes and livelihoods in this way.

Planning for asylum seekers

Global crises such as environmental disasters, civil wars and foreign invasions rarely occur completely unexpectedly. There are often warnings that they are about to happen. If the international community cannot prevent such events, it might at least be possible to prepare better for the inevitable results.

Expert View

Andrew Simms is Policy Director of the New Economics Foundation, a group that tries to think of new ways to deal with world problems:

'Defining refugee status, and the circumstances under which people should be granted the protection of another nation, has always been a controversial issue [issue for debate]. At the same time, environmental displacement has placed old definitions and categories under a huge new strain. The countries and cultures most responsible for global environmental degradation [damage] must acknowledge their role, and begin to think about policies to tackle population movement at its source. Placing new international obligations on them towards environmental refugees would help kick-start this process. These countries should understand that ignoring their neighbors is no longer an option.'

When children become refugees, they usually miss out on schooling – often for several years. These young Karen refugees from Burma (see page 30) are taking classes in a refugee camp along the Thai–Burmese border.

Host governments could make arrangements for the housing, education and medical care of asylum seekers, and discuss their arrival with the local population to reduce resentment.

International refugee organizations and individual countries could also improve the way they deal with asylum claims. Many human rights groups argue that detention centres are not suitable places for people who have experienced terrible suffering and trauma. They say that asylum seekers should be housed in the community and their claims processed quickly. It is stressful for asylum seekers to live for years in a state of limbo, not knowing if their claims will be successful.

A better reception?

At the heart of the matter is the fact that most governments see asylum seekers as a problem. This leads to negative, hostile reactions to them in society generally. If governments handle asylum seekers kindly and humanely, then it is more likely they will receive a friendly welcome. There will also be a growing understanding of why they have come and the support they need. Whether asylum seekers are welcomed or not depends on the outcome of debates in society over the issue, so each one of us has a role to play.

Glossary

aid Food, shelter or money that is given to people in need, for example, after a war.

alien From another country (a disapproving term).

asylum Protection given to people who have left their country because they were in danger.

asylum seeker A refugee who claims the right to live in safety in another country because of persecution in his or her own country.

ceasefire When enemies agree to stop fighting.

civil war A war between groups of people within the same country.

civilian A person who is not a member of the armed forces or the police.

Cold War The hostile relations between the Western powers, led by the United States, and the countries linked to the Soviet Union. It lasted from 1949 to 1990.

colony A country that is ruled over by another country.

communist Ruled like the system of government in the Soviet Union, where the government controlled the production of goods and the running of services.

convention An agreement between countries or leaders.

deported When a person is forced to go back to his or her own country.

detention centre A secure place, like a prison.

discrimination Treating one group of people in society less fairly than another group.

displaced Forced to leave home and move to another part of the country.

ethnic cleansing The policy of forcing people from a particular ethnic group to leave an area or country.

ethnic group A group of people who share a culture, tradition, way of life and sometimes language.

ethnic minority A group of people who have a different culture, religion, language or skin colour from most other people in their society.

genocide The attempt to murder everyone from a particular ethnic group.

human rights The basic rights that people have to be treated fairly, especially by their government.

humanitarian To do with reducing suffering and improving the conditions in which people live.

indigenous people The people who were the original inhabitants of a particular place, such as the Aboriginal people of Australia.

Internally Displaced Persons (IDPs) People who have been forced to leave the area where they live and move to a different part of the country.

Kurds People from Kurdistan, a region stretching mostly across Iran, Iraq, Turkey. Kurdistan is not recognized as a country.

left-wing A person with left-wing views tends to be in favour of changing society in favour of working people.

Less Economically Developed Country (LEDC) The poorer countries of the world, including the countries of Africa, Asia (except for Japan), Latin America and the Caribbean.

liberation The freedom of a country from rule by another country.

massacre The killing of a large number of people in a cruel way.

migrant Someone who moves from one region of his or her country to another, or to another country.

More Economically Developed Country (MEDC) The richer countries of the world, including Europe, North America and Australia.

NATO (North Atlantic Treaty Organization) A military organization that includes many European countries, plus the United States and Canada.

paramilitary group An armed force that is separate from the official army.

people-smuggler A person who arranges for people to travel illegally to another country.

persecution Treating people badly because of their ethnic group, culture, religious or political beliefs.

rape Forcing someone to have sex.

refugee A person who escapes to another country to seek safety from war, natural disaster or bad treatment.

refugee camp A camp built by governments or international organizations to shelter large numbers of refugees.

republic A country ruled by a president.

Roma A travelling people who originally came from India but now live mostly in Europe.

Soviet Union (USSR) The former empire, ruled from Moscow in Russia, which stretched from the Baltic and Black seas to the Pacific Ocean. It lasted from 1922 to 1991.

superpower A country that has great military or economic power and great influence. The USSR was a superpower until 1991 but since then the United States has been the world's only superpower.

trauma A mental condition caused by severe shock. Many refugees suffer trauma after their experiences.

United Nations High Commissioner for Refugees (UNHCR) An international organization set up in 1950 to protect and help refugees.

welfare system A system for giving practical help, such as money or services, to needy people.

Further information

Books

Gervelie's Story by Anthony Robinson and Annemarie Young, Frances Lincoln, 2008

Give Me Shelter: An Asylum Seeker Anthology by Tony Bradman, Frances Lincoln, 2007

Immigrants and Refugees by Cath Senker, Franklin Watts, 2004

Issues in the News: Refugees by Cath Senker, Wayland, 2008

It Happened to Me: Refugee by Angela Neustatter, Franklin Watts, 2002

Jumping to Heaven: Stories about Refugee Children by Katherine Goode, Wakefield Press, 2004

Kiss the Dust by Elizabeth Laird, Macmillan Children's Books, 2007

Refugees and Asylum Seekers by Dave Dalton, Heinemann, 2006

Refugees: We Left Because We Had To by Jill Rutter, Refugee Council, 2004

Why are People Refugees? by Cath Senker, Hodder Wayland, 2007

Websites

www.amnesty.org.uk
Amnesty International campaigns to help people worldwide who are persecuted for their beliefs.

www.itvs.org/beyondthefire
The real-life experiences of 15 teenagers who escaped from war zones and now live in the USA.

www.oxfam.org.uk/coolplanet/kidsweb/refugee/index.htm
The charity Oxfam's Cool Planet site with stories about life for refugees.

www.refugeecouncil.org.uk
The Refugee Council helps refugees and asylum seekers and campaigns for their rights. For basic information on asylum, go to http://www.refugeecouncil.org.uk/practice/basics/

www.refugeesinternational.org
A US organization that helps refugees. The site includes refugee stories.

Index

Entries in **bold** are for pictures.